north
cascades
crest

north cascades crest

crest

Notes and Images from America's Alps

James Martin

SASQUATCH BOOKS
SEATTLE

Published by Sasquatch Books.
Printed in Hong Kong by C & C Offset Printing Co., Ltd.
Distributed in Canada by Raincoast Books Ltd.
03 02 01 00 99   5 4 3 2 1

Grateful acknowledgment is made for permission to reprint the following copyrighted
material: Excerpts from "Sourdough Mountain Lookout" reprinted from *Canoeing Up
Cabarga Creek: Buddhist Poems 1955–1986* (1996) by Philip Whalen with permission of
Parallax Press, Berkeley, California. Excerpts from *Earth House Hold: Technical Notes and
Queries to Fellow Dharma Revolutionaries*, copyright 1966 by Gary Snyder. Reprinted by
permission of New Directions Publishing Corporation. Excerpts from "Mid-August at Sourdough
Mountain Lookout," from "Piute Creek," and from "Hay for the Horses" from *Riprap and Cold Mountain
Poems* by Gary Snyder.

Photograph on page 3: The Southern Pickets—Mount Terror, Mount Degenhardt, Inspiration Peak, and
the McMillan Spires—from Trapper Peak.

Book design by Karen Schober
Map illustration by Jane Shaskey
Copy editing by Don Graydon
Photograph on page 43 by James Nelson. All other photographs by the author.

Library of Congress Cataloging in Publication Data
Martin, James, 1950-
        North Cascades crest / text and photographs, James Martin.
            p. cm.
        Includes bibliographical references.
        ISBN 1-57061-140-8
        1. Mountaineering—Cascade Range. 2. Mountaineering—Washington (State) 3. Natural his-
tory—Cascade Range. 4. Natural history—Washington (State) 5. Cascade Range—Pictorial works.
6. Washington (State)—Pictorial works. I. Title.
GV199.42.C37M37 1999
796.52'2'097975—dc21   98-41006

Sasquatch Books
615 Second Avenue
Seattle, Washington 98104
(206) 467-4300
books@SasquatchBooks.com
http://www.SasquatchBooks.com

Sasquatch Books publishes high-quality adult nonfiction and children's books
related to the Northwest (Alaska to San Francisco). For more information about
our titles, contact us at the address above, or view our site on the World Wide Web.

For Art Wolfe

and Jon Krakauer, who aided and

encouraged me at the start,

and for Jim Nelson,

an ideal partner

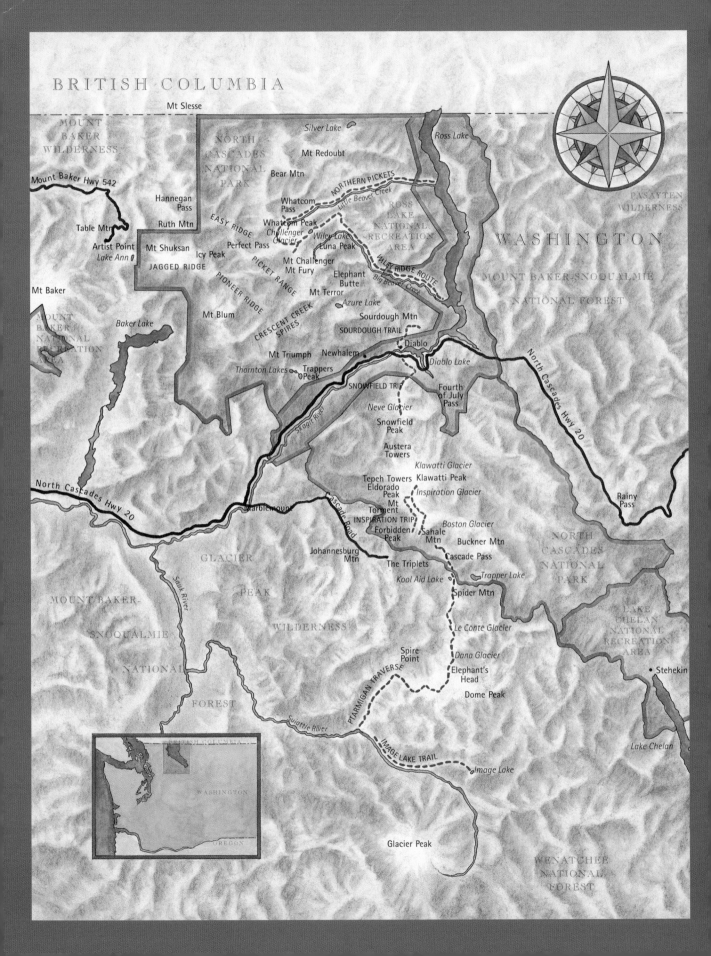

contents

Introduction

During one dismal California winter, I sought refuge from the tedium of high school life in the local library, pouring through accounts of Himalayan expeditions and dreaming over Gaston Rebuffat's photographs of the Alps. I imagined traveling through those great ranges, skirting inconceivably high walls draped in snow and ice.

Then I stumbled across Tom Miller's and Harvey Manning's *The North Cascades* (The Mountaineers, 1964, O.P.). Miller's photographs of the North Cascades crest startled me. I had imagined a Northwest carpeted by great rolling forests punctured by stately volcanic cones, but Miller's photography revealed America's own Alps, replete with the knife-edged ridges, tumbling glaciers, and spires. I loved the names: Mounts Despair and Torment, Inspiration and Forbidden Peaks, the Klawatti Icefield. The crest was still free from roads and crowds. Guarded by tangles of devil's club and precipitous approach hikes, the North Cascades exacted a price for exploring her wild places. Here was wilderness.

Six years out of high school I moved to Washington and started probing the range's defenses, conducting reconnaissances from the towering volcanoes and sorties into the temperate jungles surrounding the high country. Sometimes I reached a summit, savoring my luck for a few hours before the range revoked its hospitality. I had arrived too late to participate in the pioneering explorations of the range, which had extended into the 1950s, but I found the crest unmolested, its austere architecture protected by wilderness areas and a national park.

From my first hike I learned that the Cascades deserve their name. The sound of falling water rings everywhere. It murmurs in the forest and roars down cliffs. Tiny rivulets trace eccentric paths on the surface of glaciers, plunging into crevasses and joining one another to become

Left: *The North Cascades' abundant rainfall keeps the valley floors lush and verdant.*

torrents carrying powdered rock to the Pacific. The range harbors tremendous quantities of water in its glaciers, icecaps, and snowfields. When the warmth of summer arrives, the frozen reservoir releases its stores and the mountains sing.

Over the centuries, these waters have carved the North Cascades crest into an archipelago in the sky. Deep valleys, cut by water and ice, isolate islands of rock. Relief can exceed a vertical mile. Above tree line abides a world scoured clean by recently departed glaciers, where wildflowers glow in the brief snow-free summer, mosses snuggle between boulders, and lichens paint the stone in oranges, reds, greens, and blacks. Winds flow from the Pacific or the Arctic, usually bearing clouds that feed the glaciers and the streams. Mists swirl among the towers and form bright jewels on shimmering greenery.

Isthmuses of high ridges connect the rock islands, and for miles hikers need not dip below tree line. The great traverses of the North Cascades follow these ridges from massif to massif. You can trace a path from the Canadian border to Glacier Peak along high benches, glaciers, and ridges with only the slash of the Skagit River forcing you into deep forest. Over the years, the uninterrupted quality of the northernmost reaches of the Cascade Range called me back again and again. These grand mountains became my definition of the North Cascades crest.

For over a century, the North Cascades crest has attracted a succession of dreamers, explorers, entrepreneurs, climbers, and poets. They came in search of gold and railroad routes, adventure and beauty. Jack Kerouac and Gary Snyder sat atop Desolation Peak and Sourdough Mountain on the lookout for fire and satori. Kenneth Rexroth worked to clear the route to Cascade Pass. A host of climbers hacked their way to the hidden recesses of the range in search of first ascents and graceful lines.

The crest was protected first by topography and later by statute. At one time, developers and other exploiters threatened it directly. Miners coveted its minerals, loggers its neighboring forests. Then, in 1960, the U. S. Congress created the Glacier Peak Wilderness. Eight years later, after a campaign by the Sierra Club, the Mountaineers, and other environmental organizations, the North Cascades National Park came into existence as part of the North Cascades Act, which also included the Lake Chelan and Ross Lake National Recreation Areas and added territory to the Glacier Peak Wilderness. Today, a combination of national park and wilderness status protects the North Cascades crest from

Glacier Peak to the Canadian border, with the exception of the narrow corridor cut by State Route 20. Wilderness designation bars all vehicles and permanent improvements.

Yet, despite these protections, the crest remains threatened. The wilderness areas are too small to sustain viable ecosystems, forcing some animals, such as bears and cougars, beyond the borders. And as surrounding human populations grow more dense and encroach on the parkland boundaries, the scale is tipped against wildlife. Too frequently, increased contact between humans and wildlife yields tragic results.

The greatest immediate danger to the North Cascades crest, however, comes from those who love it best. Growing ranks of hikers and climbers scar thin carpets of vegetation with careless footsteps, tromp deer trails into deep ruts, and foul streams with their waste. The preservation and our future enjoyment of this wild landscape depends upon our recognition of its fragile nature. Wilderness travelers should try to walk primarily on rock, camp on snow instead of meadow, and carry out waste instead of burying it near streams. Enjoy the wilderness, but be a responsible steward of it as well.

With this book I have tried to convey the uniqueness of the North Cascades landscape, as well as the intimate relationship I have developed with it over the years. The book follows the crest from the Canadian border to Glacier Peak, pausing to consider both natural and human history. Because I love spectacular scenery, I included major peaks adjacent to the crest proper. Thus, I classify Mount Slesse as part of the crest by virtue of its nonpareil north face and spectacular profile. Mount Baker gains entrance because of its prominence and the role of volcanoes in creating the crest. My classification is personal.

I've tried to capture on film those singular moments of transcendence wilderness bestows without warning, when light and form intersect in ways that jar me from my day-to-day seeing. Such moments occur every day on the crest, available to anyone paying attention. These are part of the unquantifiable values of wild lands. Thoreau wrote that in wildness is the preservation of the world. On the North Cascades crest we can still make contact with wildness. I couldn't live without it.

A Walk to the Crest

"At times it

seems the ice age ended

only yesterday."

CHAPTER

a walk to the crest

Every journey to the North Cascades crest follows a sequence. Each trail or route moves vertically from evergreen forests to terrain more common to the Arctic Circle; each trek ascends from a realm of abundant life to a rocky landscape of boreal austerity. At times it seems the ice age ended only yesterday. Glacier polish still shines.

Even the forests are new. Just a few thousand years ago ice chased both people and trees out of the valleys. After millennia of gouging and planing, the ice retreated. The evergreen forest began anew, reclaiming the soil and reestablishing the ecosystem in a geological blink. In the tropics, rain forests developed over millions of years, permitting vast numbers of species to forge an incomprehensibly elaborate web of diversity and interrelationships. By comparison, the temperate forests of the Northwest are mere sketches. Even so, tracing the interlocking dependencies within a single acre of our rudimentary forest may forever remain a challenge.

On a windless morning, I shouldered my pack and lit out toward Torment Basin, the silence disturbed only by the Cascade River's music and the groan and crack of tiny glaciers perched on rocky bowls high above. Droplets of water quivered at the tip of each thistle needle and pooled atop huckleberry leaves. Spiders and beetles worked below the threshold of hearing. Deep in the forest, moss draperies blocked the valley's dim light. Humus sopped up the thud of my footfalls.

Thickets of devil's club glowered, guarding either side of shallow streams. Bouquets of red berries dangled at their tops. Their broad, flat leaves appeared furred, hiding cruel barbs along the branches. I bypassed each of these briar patches or hiked over them on fallen logs.

Hours passed as I gained elevation, and then the forest ended abruptly as if the trees beyond this point had been mown down by a scythe. Gardens filled the bottom of Torment Basin, ringed by moraines, scoured rock, and living ice. The glaciers had pulsed to tree line a few generations ago, but life recaptured the terrain as the ice withdrew. Now, gaudy flowers crowd the brooks—monkey flower, paintbrush, gentian, columbine. Heather holds sandy moraines together, its pink and white bells shivering in a breath of breeze.

The clouds thinned. Across the valley the mute, cloud-shrouded buttresses of Johannesburg Mountain waited like ghosts. Creeks slalomed down the hillsides, quicksilver strands woven through the forest, while above the swatch of dark greens, cloud and rock spoke in a lexicon of grays. A cold breeze streamed from the glaciers, an echo of katabatic winds that howled when ice held sway. I could feel the Pleistocene on my face.

Right: *Glacier ice blankets the north side of Mount Challenger in the Pickets.*

As I walked alone, the city chatter of my mind subsided. I felt the rhythms of living here—the pace of my steps, the beat of my heart, the cadence of my breath. I could sense glaciers advancing and retreating like sine waves. Deeper, the mountains breathe, too, ever so slowly. We live in an inhalation of their breath. We watch the spin of seasons,

while far below swings the tectonic rising and erosional subsiding of the Cascade crest itself.

Clouds swallowed the peaks again. As I set up my tent amid morainal rubble, mist coagulated around me. I settled into my shelter and gnawed on my dinner—no need for the noise and distraction of a stove.

Fatigue flattened me, and aches isolated each bundle of muscle. The backcountry will acquaint you with many ailments that flesh is heir to: blisters, exfoliating toenails, plantar fascitis, bunions, turned ankles, bad knees, bleeding hips, tweaked backs; skin punctured and inflamed by mosquitoes, chomped by flies, scourged by devil's club, stung by nettles, and burned by the sun; innards suffering from dehydration, altitude sickness, and symptomatic of giardia, gas. Given the possibilities, the soreness of that night felt like a blessing.

As I fell asleep, the wind kicked up. A driven mist began hissing, and before sunrise rain tapped a tabla solo on the rain fly. As I shed my bag, the rain abated and the scene brightened. I saw the sun's disc through the clouds, with wet, black rock shimmering and heather-mantled ridges glowing in muted light like backlit emeralds.

I saw my target, a prominence near the summit of Mount Torment at the far end of a thin curving ridge cupping an icy snowfield. I scrambled over talus, ready to leap when blocks gave way under my feet.

When I gained the ridge, I was treated to a new vista, another vertiginous prospect overlooking a forest of peaks above Inspiration Icefield. I paused to soak in the view before negotiating the ridge. Towers blocked my progress, forcing me to weave around them on either side or attack them directly. Even on easy ground, movement here demands perfect attention.

On the prominence the only signs of life were the dull-colored mats of lichens eating their way through rock. The sky became a limitless azure dome while fog filled the valleys utterly. Only ragged black spires and brilliant snow domes pierced the blanket of billowy white. The fog muffled all sound, and I sat in silence surrounded by peaks without number.

Previous page: *A tranquil stretch of the Nooksack River.*

Right: *Jim Nelson descends Sharkfin Tower after working on a new route.*

Rock: Northern Peaks

"The entire prospect

to the south is a maze of

spire and ice. . . ."

CHAPTER

2

rock: northern peaks

Small and swampy, Depot Creek crosses the U.S.-Canadian border a few miles from Chilliwack Lake, British Columbia. Just to the south of this modest border crossing, in Washington state, stands Mount Redoubt, a prototypical Cascade peak with a cleft in the loose black rock on its north face filled with living ice. The glacier leads to a high pass between Redoubt and Mox Peaks (known to climbers as Twin Spires). Here one passes into a new world, shining from recent glacial scrubbings. This is the crest of the North Cascades.

From the pass, the snowy dome of Mount Spickard rises in the north-east. Look in the opposite direction to view the sheer curving north wall of Bear Mountain brooding in shadow. Farther south lie the Pickets, the most rugged mountains in the Lower 48 states. The entire prospect to the south is a maze of spire and ice, uncountable heights in dizzy profusion dominated by the distant cone of Glacier Peak. If you travel the crest south, you cross only one trail and follow none from here to the far side of the Pickets. And anyone tracing the crest all the way to Glacier Peak need cross only one road—State Route 20, the North Cascades Highway. Stepping over the shoulder of Redoubt takes one into a wilderness that welcomes fewer visitors than the Pickets themselves.

Amid the abundance of striking peaks sits Ruth Mountain, an unassuming rounded summit between Mount Shuksan and the Chilliwack River. Close enough to the road for a day hike and requiring only rudimentary mountaineering skills, Ruth affords an expansive and instructive view of the North Cascades. From the summit of Ruth, Cascade geology lies exposed and summarized, but one reads a palimpsest, not an essay. Time has erased, snipped, covered, twisted, and rearranged the text. This is no Grand Canyon geological layer cake where the trail zigzags down through time from the Cenozoic to the Precambrian. Instead, the Cascades are a lithic bouillabaisse: granitic bubbles and simmering volcanoes in a matrix of tortured metamorphics and loose sedimentaries. Their story is violent and improbable.

If you're looking for the origins of the North Cascades, the middle of the Atlantic Ocean is a good place to start. At one time all the continents cohered in a single landmass called Pangaea. But some 200 million years ago this supercontinent began breaking up. The continents rode apart on tectonic plates, relatively buoyant crusts that float atop denser rock.

The primary engine for the continental breakup was the emerging Atlantic Ocean. An oceanic ridge split apart and then filled with magma—superheated liquid rock. The magma cooled to become basalt and thus new oceanic crust was born, in a process called seafloor spreading. The Atlantic averaged a few inches of growth per year, eventually prying Europe from North America, and Africa from South America. Bits of continental crust called microcontinents broke off from the main plates. For example, the island of Madagascar is a microcontinent fragment broken from Africa's plate.

As the Atlantic expanded, it pushed the North American plate westward into the Pacific plate. The western edge of North America crumpled like a fender, but in the process known as subduction, the heavier rock of the Pacific plate dove under the North American plate for 60 to 100 miles. The initial wrinkling of the North American plate caused the first rising of the Rocky Mountains into coastal peaks reaching as high as 20,000 feet.

At the same time, microcontinents and volcanic islands moved

Left: *The spine of the North Cascades crest is composed of tortured metamorphic rock.*

toward North America on a conveyor belt of oceanic crust and began colliding with the western coast. These masses didn't subduct under the North American plate because they consisted of lighter material. Instead, they floated to become part of the continent.

Ninety to one hundred million years ago, a group of islands that were to become the North Cascades piled up against the North American plate. The collision created horizontal faults that thrust and sheared the islands into thin slices, overlapping one another like a deck of cards. Much later, tectonic forces shifted their movement north and shaved them into thin strips. The North Cascades remain a series of north-south parallel belts bounded by faults, all moving north.

The ancestral components of the North Cascades traveled a long way. Magnetic data in the rock indicates they came from the equator, and shallow marine limestones found in the range contain fossils of a clam found only in Asia. Much of the rock in the North Cascades migrated about 4,400 miles. Horizontal faulting and partial subduction metamorphosed most of it—that is, altered its structure by heating and compressing—before uplifting and erosion exposed the reborn rock.

The bulk of the crest is composed of rocks known collectively as the Skagit metamorphic suite: gneisses and schists that once were granite, volcanic ash, sandstone, or serpentine, but that underwent metamorphism 60 to 90 million years ago. The Skagit suite is the crystalline backbone of the range. The view from Ruth Mountain of the great wall of the Pickets shows Skagit gneiss to advantage. South of the Pickets, the peaks of Snowfield, Buckner, and Forbidden are prominent examples of the suite. Beyond the Northern Pickets rise the summits near Hozomeen Mountain, composed of greenstone, which is metamorphosed basalt.

To the west of Ruth, Mount Shuksan displays greenschist peppered with lawsonite and aragonite, minerals that form only when buried at least twelve miles beneath the surface. Due north along the Canadian border the peaks exhibit the Chilliwack formation, ancient fossiliferous limestone and other sedimentary rock of the late Permian period, which ended 225 million years ago. The peaks north of Mount Baker are sedimentary as well, but much younger—only 120 to 150 million years old.

When magma cools within the earth and the chemical composition is just right, bodies of granitic rock form. Small bubbles of granite are called plutons, or stocks, while larger intrusions are called batholiths.

Right: *The moon sets at dusk above Mount Baker and Mount Shuksan.*

Because granitic rock tends to be firm and monolithic, it weathers well. Climbers seek out plutons and batholiths because holds don't break off in the hand and fewer rocks fall from above.

The summit of Ruth Mountain is ringed by peaks carved out of the Chilliwack Batholith. Slesse's fang, Bear's arcing wall, Challenger's broad shoulders, and Blum's broad nose consist of various diorites, a type of granitic rock, from the Chilliwack. The batholith runs from the north shore of Chilliwack Lake south to State Route 20, squeezed between the

Pickets and Shuksan. Near the lower end of the North Cascades, just south of Dome Peak, is the high point for the Cloudy Pass Batholith, 100 square miles of granitic rock. Here and there small plutons show themselves, a few sharp white teeth amid relative rubble.

The same slow tectonic movement that transported equatorial islands to the Pacific Northwest also cracked the skin of the North American plate and created a chain of volcanoes 35 to 40 million years ago. These Western Cascade volcanoes grew on an arch created by pressure from a sea of magma far below—magma formed by the intense stress of the Pacific plate slipping beneath the North American plate. When the magma cooled and shrank about 17 million years ago, the pressure on the arch subsided and the volcanoes, now dead, dropped between faults. Erosion and new eruptions then conspired to hide almost all traces of the ancient Western Cascades.

Twelve million years ago, the Cascade volcanoes reawakened. The continuing subduction of the seafloor with the North American plate fed magma to the nascent cones. The entire chain sat east of the former Western Cascades and atop the remains of their relict arch. A new arch pushed the entire range skyward. Although volcanism resumed millions of years ago, the mountains we see today are much younger because erosion and new eruptions again leveled and concealed almost all traces of the earlier mountains.

The present chain of Cascade volcanoes, dubbed the High Cascades, runs south from Mount Garibaldi in British Columbia to Mount Lassen in California. From the summit of Mount Rainier one can see Baker, Glacier, St. Helens, Adams, Hood, and Jefferson, each volcano the highest peak in its area.

Glacier Peak is the oldest and least active modern Cascades cone. It began building about 750,000 years ago and last erupted more than 11,000 years ago. Because the volcano added no new rock in eleven millennia, its glaciers eroded it deeply. Mount Baker, where lava flowed less than a thousand years ago, shows less erosion despite its larger glaciers. Baker's present cone started to grow about 400,000 years ago.

The Cascades are full of dormant or extinct volcanoes, and most will remain that way. Oregon's Three Fingered Jack is unlikely to resurrect itself and restore its profound wasting. But volcanic action in the range is far from over. On August 17, 1870, during the first known ascent of Mount Rainier, Hazard Stevens and Philemon Beecher Van Trump

Left: *Early autumn snow dusts the summit of Mount Shuksan.*

Following page: *Nooksack Tower, Price Glacier, and Mount Shuksan loom over hidden Price Lake.*

found shelter overnight on the summit in a volcanic steam cave. In the late 1970s Mount Baker began spewing steam. Hot springs bubbled suspiciously on the flanks of Glacier Peak. And on May 18, 1980, Mount St. Helens blew its top in a cataclysmic eruption. The range clearly is alive and well, ready to spring new surprises.

Volcanoes are inherently violent. At minimum they leak viscous magma. In the interval between building the Western and High Cascades, volcanic action covered tens of thousands of miles in basalt. Some of the volcanoes exploded like Mount St. Helens did in 1980. Stratigraphers have found ash from ancient Cascade eruptions in the Dakotas and beyond. And the North Cascades have had their share of violent events.

Lake Ann is a little jewel nestled on a bench between Baker and Shuksan. Below the bench is the epicenter of a great explosion, an area now called the Kulshan caldera. About 1.1 million years ago, a volcano overlain with glacial ice collapsed, triggering a massive explosion, like Mount Mazama detonating to create Crater Lake in southern Oregon. The ice instantly turned to steam, increasing the force of the blast. It left a four-mile- by five-mile-wide crater. This was a Krakatoa-sized eruption; when that Indonesian volcano erupted in the late nineteenth century, ash dimmed the sun and temperatures dipped worldwide. Meteorologists in Europe attributed three successive record-breaking cold winters to ash in the atmosphere. The Kulshan explosion deposited ash 3,000 feet deep, enough to bury Yosemite Valley, but glaciers have since scraped away most of the evidence.

The story of the birth and upbringing of the North Cascades is still unclear and subject to revision. At a glance, we see only the surface of the picture, and even that is tortured and deformed. The three-dimensional checkerboard of faults riven with molten intrusions is yet to be reconstructed perfectly. Parts of the puzzle have disappeared, stripped away by glaciers, blown to bits by eruptions, or thrust aloft for wind and weather to disperse. Much of the mystery of these mountains may outlive us all.

The Pickets: Echoes of Beckey

"We had thousands

of feet of air under our heels,

and the packs tugged

us into space."

CHAPTER

3

the pickets: echoes of beckey

On the second day of the trip to the Northern Pickets, Jim Nelson and I climbed a small knoll above Whatcom Pass and searched for a route to the far side of Mount Challenger. Jim was a good man to be with. Over the past two decades, no one had equaled his record of high-quality first ascents and first winter ascents in the North Cascades. When not climbing on his own, he worked as a guide or in a climbing shop, and he co-authored *Selected Climbs in the Cascades* with Peter Potterfield. Only the legendary Fred Beckey, who first trod this ground more than half a century ago, has a deeper history with the range.

We spied two routes to Challenger. Dropping under the shoulder of Whatcom Peak offered the most direct access, but a retreating glacier had left debris and polished rock in its wake that would make travel tedious and somewhat dangerous. We decided instead to reach Challenger by climbing up and over Whatcom. Talus and snow slopes ran most of the way up Whatcom's north face. We would head up that mountain the next day and camp near the summit. We wanted views.

We descended to a campsite west of the pass, out of the wind but also away from the view. A small creek garlanded in monkey flowers compensated for the loss. Although we sat midway on the main trail across the northern range, no one disturbed our solitude.

The next day dawned clear. Hefting our packs, still heavy with food so early in the trip, we ascended easy terrain toward the headwall on Whatcom's north flank. As the route steepened, loose scree supplanted snow and boulders. Jim started traversing west on dirty benches to skirt the headwall. Loose rock covered the benches and climbing to the next-higher bench required total focus. We had thousands of feet of air under our heels, and the packs tugged us into space. Although the route never exceeded third class in difficulty, the unroped exposure made it more dangerous than the hardest fifth-class rock climb protected by ropes. Jim sped ahead as usual, sparing me the effort of route finding. We topped out at a low pass between Whatcom's summit and the ridge dipping toward Perfect Pass, a tempting but ultimately disappointing name for a route requiring ropes.

We set up the tent on a hump of snow and the kitchen in the moat between snow and rock. We scrambled to the summit, a mere fifteen-minute romp, to plan our sunset pictures and get the lay of the land. Challenger Glacier gleamed in afternoon light. The empty country surrounding Mount Blum lay below, and the southern horizon teemed with peaks. Shuksan and Baker loomed darkly in the west. We hoped the wisping clouds wouldn't build and blot out the sunset. After an hour's study of the view, we descended for naps and an early dinner.

When the sun dipped near the horizon, we headed back to the summit. The clouds swirled, gathering color above mountains silhouetted to the west. A cold breeze chilled us, and we felt utterly alone. Darkness smothered the last of the tints and cold gripped the high country, driving us back to camp.

Right: *James Martin and Fred Beckey after completing a first ascent in Canada's Coast Range.*

Following page: *Glaciers scrubbed and gouged the terrain around Trapper Lakes in the recent geologic past.*

Dawn found us on the summit again, but clouds in the northeast deprived us of a sunrise show. We couldn't work up any disappointment. The sun broke above the gray layer and warmed the slopes. We struck camp, skidded down to Perfect Pass, and down-climbed to Challenger Glacier. At the last, the ropes came out. Crevasses scarred the glacier but the route was obvious. Bright sun bounced on the ice and glared under the brims of our hats. We covered our necks with handkerchiefs. In a couple of hours, we established camp on a moraine on the glacier's far side.

At this camp, the midpoint of our journey, I noticed that the heel of one boot was separating from the sole. One of Jim's had detached at the same time. I thought we were doomed to limp out of the range, but Jim reached into his bag of doodads and pulled out tiny packages of epoxy. We devoted the afternoon to cleaning the boots, applying the epoxy, and standing motionless to allow it to set. Another party joined us on our moraine, a bit puzzled why two men stood like statues facing Challenger, each wearing only one boot.

The next day we climbed Challenger. The rangers had warned us that the moat was impassable, but the step across from snow to rock confirmed our opinion of secondhand information. One moderate technical pitch brought us to the top. The Pickets spread out below us. A great wall curved from our peak to Mount Fury, spiked by the summits of Crooked Thumb, Ghost, Phantom, and Swiss Peaks. The prickly Southern Pickets peered over these north faces. To the east, we could see the chocolate waters of Luna Lake sparkling with light as wind rippled its surface.

Haze and clouds were building while mist churned below Challenger's cliffy south wall. The weather was changing. We scooted back to camp, packed, and moved to the high point of Wiley Ridge, where we found a garden of grass, flowers, and lichen. The north face of Fury rumbled with falling ice and rock. The summit of Challenger vanished as clouds gathered and gave us a good dousing.

We spent the following day on prime ridge land. We paused next to lakes, still half-frozen in August, and whiled away hours fiddling with our photography. By late afternoon a cozy bench suggested itself for camp. Seduced by flat, soft ground, we dropped our packs for the remains of the day.

We saw rain streaming over Swiss Peak as we wolfed breakfast the next morning. Time to run. We had shouldered our packs by the time the rain hit and soon were sidehilling along faint paths and plowing straight through sopping heather. As the angle rose, the footing became treacherous. Jim ordered a halt to put on crampons. The crampons kept our boots from slipping, but our ankles felt the strain. As the ridge sloped toward Beaver Pass, we lost the track. Our first guess led us up to an impasse. We began losing altitude with the second guess. The crampons came off. The path vanished again, and we pounded through slide alder and climbed down roots to bypass cliffs. The rain continued. Every leaf unloaded water droplets on us. The unrelenting grade jammed our toes in our boots. We slipped when the skin of the hillside gave way. I struggled to keep up with Jim. After an age, the angle moderated. Half an hour of easy huckleberry country then brought us to Beaver Pass and the very welcome trail to Ross Lake.

My weary body and battered feet cried for rest, but we needed to meet our boat the next morning. After miles of gritting my teeth and negotiating with pain, the sight of Jim pulling off the trail for the night gladdened my heart. It was a sodden camp. I was soaked. My feet were blistered and torn—soon two toenails would blacken and fall off. I didn't care; I could languish undisturbed until morning.

The next day, only four hours of misery remained, not counting the last slow mile of uphill to the car after the Ross Lake boat deposited us below the North Cascades Highway. We piled into the car and found the battery dead. But nothing could dampen our spirits. The weather had cooperated at critical times, and anyway, we had expected a beating in the Pickets. Then a good Samaritan gave us a jump-start.

I presented a pathetic picture as I hobbled around packing the car and pulling my tired bones inside. After all, this had been an easy trip. We had followed good trail most of the way, and a climbers' path showed us the easiest route across heather and through brush most of the time. As I drove, I couldn't help but think of Fred Beckey and his younger brother, Helmy, exploring the range in 1940, bagging the first ascents of McMillan, Phantom, Inspiration, and Crooked Thumb along the way—teenagers armed only with army surplus gear, faulty maps, and gobs of enthusiasm.

In the summer of 1939 Fred Beckey was a member of the first party ever to reach the top of Mount Despair—one of thirty-five summits the teenager stood upon that year and his initial first ascent. He was the puppy of the trip. Veteran climber Lloyd Anderson—one of the founders of Recreational Equipment Incorporated (REI)—had noticed the talent and drive of young Beckey on training climbs sponsored by the Mountaineers Club and invited him on an assault of the isolated peak southwest of the Southern Pickets. Don't imagine them strolling up a trail. In those days North Cascades climbers hacked their way through jungle while wearing wood-frame packs and carrying heavy, primitive gear. Despite the effort, mountaineering enthralled Beckey from the first.

From the summit of Despair, Beckey saw the Picket Range up close for the first time. The Pickets described a W in stone carved by the glaciers that once filled the valleys of Luna and McMillan Creeks. Thickets of alder and devil's club smothered the valley floors, while pocket glaciers perched uncertainly on steep cirque walls. The great barricade of the Southern Pickets bristled with towers and spires.

Fired with youthful enthusiasm, Fred and Helmy decided to explore the Pickets the following summer, traversing the most rugged region of the Cascades alone. Only one party had ever approached the range by their intended route, and many major summits remained unclimbed. Undeterred by prudence, they shouldered sixty-five-pound packs on July 7, 1940, and hiked over Hannegan Pass to camp by the Chilliwack River.

The next morning they climbed out of the Chilliwack valley. No trail zigzagged up the misnamed Easy Ridge or over the justly named Perfect Pass. A jumble of ridges and valleys greeted them when they burst above tree line. They started by climbing Whatcom Peak, then decided they could sort out the chaotic terrain from the top of Challenger. By the morning of the fourth day, they stood on the summit of Challenger— only its third ascent—with the Pickets spread below them like a relief map. Gentle Luna stood apart, while the steep north wall of Fury rose unmolested. A serrated ridge curved from Fury back to Challenger.

One unclimbed fang on the ridge beckoned the brothers. Dubbing the peak Crooked Thumb, they looked for weaknesses in its defenses on the west slope. Rotten, slabby rock thwarted them until they encountered a finger of hard snow breaking the face. They delicately chopped steps up the snow to a rock rib, where they donned tennis shoes for the summit push. Treading carefully on loose rock, the boys climbed the final four hundred feet to the top for first-ascent No. 1 of the trip.

Elated, the lads crossed over Challenger Arm and traversed to the milky tarn of Luna Lake, nestled beneath Fury's north face. The view from camp dazzled Fred. Avalanches and thunder echoed in the cirque. In his autobiographical *Challenge of the North Cascades*, he wrote, "The icy armor of the eastern faces of Challenger, Crooked Thumb, and the peak we were to call Phantom present perhaps the most splendid wall in the Cascades."

After dashing up Luna and toiling up Fury the next drizzling day, the boys were surprised to find people at their lakeside camp. The lake had seen visitors only once before, and no other party would travel to Luna Lake again for ten more years. Will Thompson, who had visited the lake in 1937 and made the first ascent of Fury, had followed the Beckey brothers over Challenger Glacier with two companions.

With food dwindling, the boys said farewell to their visitors and set their sights on Phantom, now the area's most impressive unclimbed summit. Bracketed by Fury and Crooked Thumb, Phantom presented

Right: *Above the clouds on Wiley Ridge in the Northern Pickets.*

few technical problems but many hazards. They made short work of the broken glacier and steep couloir leading to the ridge top despite stifling heat and nearby avalanches. After negotiating an airy knife-edged ridge, they paused atop their first-ascent No. 2.

Beckey later recalled that trip as "one of the roughest. I think we were very bold doing our first major climbs in desperate country." But not content with one adventure in the Pickets, the boys returned two months later, this time to the Southern Pickets. They aimed to climb Inspiration Peak and McMillan Spire. After a hellish approach hike beside Terror Creek, they achieved both summits in a single day, both first ascents.

In the ensuing years, Fred Beckey became the most prolific moun-taineer in history. Steck and Roper's *Fifty Classic Climbs in North America* lists four routes in the North Cascades: The climbs on Forbidden, Shuksan, and Slesse are Beckey first-ascent routes, and he made the first ascent of Liberty Bell by another line. He found gems in every corner of the range. There isn't a five-mile stretch along the crest without a Beckey route. "I don't know why I've done so many first ascents," Beckey once mused. "I guess I like the sense of adventure, the unknown, and the need for self-reliance."

Beckey applied the lessons he learned in the nursery of the Pickets to the other great ranges of North America. Open a guidebook to any major climbing area on the continent; his name leaps from the pages. He studied each region—his voracious eye quick to recognize unclimbed treasure— and then plundered them with the thoroughness of Tamerlane sacking Asia Minor.

Beckey opened the golden age of climbing on the north walls of the Canadian Rockies. On a multiday ascent in the Bugaboos, he applied Yosemite-style techniques to a North American alpine climb for the first time: direct-aid climbing, hauling loads up vertical faces, sleeping suspended in hammocks. Not content to enjoy the pleasures of summer, Beckey completed the first winter ascents of the highest peaks in the Canadian Rockies and Selkirks, enterprises that risked minus fifty-degree temperatures and deadly winds. In the American Southwest, Beckey was among the first to tap the climbing potential of the sand-stone monuments.

Beckey's 1954 trip to Alaska with Heinrich Harrer and Henry Meybohm resulted in the creation of the third route on Denali (Mount McKinley) and the first ascent of nearby Mounts Hunter and Deborah. The men called the ascent of Deborah "the most spectacular climb" any of them had ever done. Considering that Harrer (author of *Seven Years in Tibet*) had been a member of the first team to climb the north face of the Eiger and that Beckey had already completed many formidable climbs, these were strong words. "I suppose it was a lot of climbing for one summer," Beckey said, "but it didn't seem so at the time."

Beckey ruined the first-ascent game for much of the rest of the world. He snatched the plums, then busied himself with a mopping-up opera-tion. Ambitious mountaineers were reduced to looking for the cracks between his climbs. Wonderful climbing possibilities remain: severe

Left: *Glaciers are still carving the east wall of the Luna Creek amphitheater in the Northern Pickets.*

routes on 8,000-meter Himalayan giants and overhanging test pieces beyond the ability of anyone living today. But the wholesale pillage of entire regions can't happen again on this earth. The next Fred Beckey will climb the mountains of Mars.

Beckey annotated his exploits in a flurry of articles, books, and guides. His latest effort, *The Range of Glaciers: The Exploration and Survey of Northern Cascade Range* (1999), traces the early exploration of the Cascades. He brings the same appetite for knowledge to his scholarly work as to his climbing, chasing leads in university libraries and through volumes of old correspondence. His prose echoes the Victorian style of his sources. He laced his climbing guide to the Cascades, known to mountaineers as Beckey's Bible, with encyclopedic notes on history, geology, and biology. A slender pocket book in its 1949 incarnation, his *Cascade Alpine Guide* later swelled to three thick volumes. No other climbing guide demonstrates such exhaustive mastery of place.

Beckey's *Challenge of the North Cascades* concludes with his 1968 return to the North Cascades for the ascent of a new route on Bear Mountain, a giant peak north of the Pickets. From the summit Beckey was surrounded by the mountains he knew best. He could see the Pickets to the southwest, site of seven of his first ascents. To the northwest, in British Columbia, stood his most impressive Cascades route, the northeast buttress of Slesse Mountain.

At that point, after thirty years of first ascents, Beckey could have retired to bask in glory. But the following decades continued to fill with climbs at the same breakneck pace. Today's climbers armed with guidebooks and modern gear can only marvel, as we did after our ascent of Challenger, at this record of single-minded achievement.

Right: *Looking across the Skagit River Valley from Trapper Peak.*

Lookouts: Poets and Monks

"[He] kept a vigil

for fires and enlightenment

on Sourdough Mountain."

CHAPTER 4

lookouts: poets and monks

The trail to the Sourdough Mountain fire lookout switchbacks above Diablo Dam, one of three dams confining the Skagit River. The dam sits in one of the deepest canyons in North America if you measure from the Skagit to the summits on either side. The Sourdough trail climbs a vertical mile to the lookout, and the surrounding peaks tower above it.

In early summer the south-facing trail broils from midmorning to late afternoon. Ascending the trail one day, I dawdled, waiting for the sun to drift north and west. I hiked through thin forest up the relentless grade, my skin reddening in the heat for a couple of hours until I entered a shady zone. To my happy surprise, I found running water about halfway up the hill. Hikers often will find only one creek running—and that a mere hour from the top. I was traveling light so my misery index was low.

By sunset I reached the top of Stetattle Ridge, a mile-high whaleback between the dam and McMillan Creek. From my vantage point, the lookout sat on a knoll to the east, an undistinguished knob at the end of the ridge. To the west the ridge ended abruptly at the Southern Pickets, with towering East McMillan Spire blocking progress and a cluster of needles and fangs crowding behind it. The route to McMillan cruises across meadows and lightly forested benches with only Elephant Butte to slow traverses until the Pickets elevate the level of difficulty and commitment.

I saved the Pickets for another day. In a quarter-hour I arrived at the Sourdough lookout, which is now a counterculture shrine as well as a hikers' destination. A braid of circumstance ties the Beat Generation to the North Cascades crest. In the early 1950s, a weary America turned its attention to getting ahead after enduring the Depression and World War II—and in that era of the man in the gray flannel suit, a group of literary rebels hit the road and the trail. While the Lost Generation found its refuge and inspiration in Paris, the beats found their safe harbor in the North Cascades as well as in San Francisco's North Beach.

Decades before tutoring the young lions of beat literature in his San Francisco study, polymath Kenneth Rexroth helped maintain the Cascade Pass trail. Before winning the Pulitzer Prize for poetry, Gary Snyder worked trail crew and kept a vigil for fires and enlightenment on Sourdough Mountain. Philip Whalen meditated on Sauk Mountain. And Jack Kerouac enjoyed a couple of cleansing months off the road manning the Desolation Peak lookout, gazing into the Pickets and north to Hozomeen Mountain, before fame and booze snuffed him out.

Kenneth Rexroth ran point for the beats. He moved from the flatlands of Indiana in 1924. He had steeped himself in language and literature, aligned himself with the Wobblies and other political radicals, operated a bohemian coffee house, and pursued a career as an artist, all before turning twenty-one. His reputation rests on his poetry and criticism, volumes filled with the erudition and crankiness of Ezra Pound informed by deep humanity. General readers know him for his essays on classic literature in the *Saturday Review*.

This product of the Eastern intelligentsia found the North Cascades en route to San Francisco. He was a fit and active young man with smoldering eyes. Even then he was known to be intense and impatient with ignorance and stupidity, yet he felt at home among the Forest Service packers and crew who called him the Chicago Kid. Rexroth spent weeks alone chopping out downfall, repairing riprap, fashioning bridges, and clearing brush. In those days the backcountry attracted miners, hunters, and a few crazies instead of hikers and climbers. He fled the high country when a deranged hermit threatened him with a rifle for reasons Rexroth couldn't fathom.

By the 1950s Rexroth was a fixture in the San Francisco literary scene. He organized the famous Six Gallery poetry reading in 1955, where Allen Ginsberg read *Howl* for the first time like a queer, desert-mad Old Testament prophet, stunning the audience of 150 in the former auto shop and rocketing the beats onto the radar screen of popular culture.

Gary Snyder read at the Six Gallery, too. Snyder was a recent graduate of Oregon's Reed College, where he studied poetry and Zen Buddhism with his roommate Phil Whalen while completing his nominal major, anthropology.

In the early fifties, both Whalen and Snyder took summer jobs as fire lookouts on mountains above the Skagit River. In those years Whalen spent summers at Desolation, Sauk, and Sourdough, the last serving as inspiration and title for his poem "Sourdough Mountain Lookout":

> *Then I'm alone in a glass house on a ridge*
> *Encircled by chiming mountains*
> *With one sun roaring through the house all day*
> *& the others crashing through the walls all night*

And later in the poem:

> *What we see of the world is the mind's*
> *Invention and the mind*
> *Though stained by it, becoming*
> *Rivers, sun, mule-dung, flies-*

Gary Snyder documented summers on the Sourdough and Crater lookouts in *Earth House Hold*, a unique compendium of journal entries, translations, and essays. His time on the mountaintops informs most of his books, including *Riprap & Cold Mountain Poems*, *The Back Country*,

Following page: *From Sourdough Ridge, Mount Buckner and the Boston Glacier (left of center) peer over the shoulder of Pyramid Peak.*

and *Mountains and Rivers Without End*, the magnum opus he polished for forty years. Snyder won a Pulitzer Prize for *No Nature* in the 1970s.

I first read about Snyder in Kerouac's fictional memoir *The Dharma Bums*, where he was thinly disguised as the character Japhy Ryder, a Zen mountaineer. Then in the turbulent year of 1968 I fled the assassinations, the war, and the stifling oppression of high school toward the life-affirming yet naïve dreams circulating in Berkeley and in San Francisco's Haight-Ashbury. One day I opened an issue of the *San Francisco Oracle* featuring a conversation between Allen Ginsberg, Timothy Leary, and Gary Snyder. Snyder's Buddhist/naturalist world-view struck a chord so I tracked down his books. His words fit my soul as if a special place had been carved for them.

A photo on the opening page of *Riprap & Cold Mountain Poems* showed Snyder at the door of the Sourdough lookout in 1953, and the closing lines of the first poem, "Mid-August at Sourdough Mountain Lookout," evinced the serenity and the be-here-now attention that mountains brought to me:

> *Drinking cold snow-water from a tin cup*
> *Looking down for miles*
> *Through the high still air.*

"Hay for the Horses" reinforced my adolescent determination to reject the paths others thought best for me. It concludes with these frightening lines:

> *"I'm sixty-eight" he said,*
> *"I first bucked hay when I was seventeen.*
> *I thought, that day I started,*
> *I sure would hate to do this all my life.*
> *And dammit, that's just what*
> *I've gone and done."*

"Piute Creek" evoked the nameless state of being I sought:

> *Words and books*
> *Like a small creek off a high ledge*
> *Gone in the dry air.*

That summer I organized a 350-mile hike in the Sierra Nevadas of California, and from that time the trajectory of my life was fixed. The following summer, after high school graduation, I hitched alone to the Sierras to visit Piute Creek. As I rested at a pass, a miracle occurred: Gary Snyder appeared on the trail, heading my way carrying an old Trapper Nelson wood pack upholstered with a badger skin. It got better.

Snyder and his four friends invited me to accompany them on their loop hike through northern Kings Canyon National Park.

One day Snyder and I walked around the shore of Evolution Lake together, speaking of Thoreau and Muir, two saintly fools and wilderness apostles. Snyder spoke of his years in a Japanese Zen monastery and working on a tramp steamer, laboring on trail crews in the mountains of the west and climbing in the Cascades, how Rexroth influenced him and why Kerouac's Japhy Ryder character embarrassed him. And he remembered Sourdough.

I returned home renewed, believing for the first time that I could live as I saw fit. All the things I cherished—mountains, solitude, literature, transcendence—became achievable once I knew that others live uncompromised lives. I resolved to spend my life walking to and fro in the mountains, and to sit atop Sourdough one day.

I found a copy of *Earth House Hold* and carried it with me for years. *Earth House Hold* combines clean observation with significant and often humorous detail: "So many mountains, on so clear a day, the mind is staggered, and so looks to little things like pilot bread and cheese and bits of dried fruit. From Canada to Oregon, and the ranges both east and west—the blue mass of the Olympics far over hazy Puget Sound—'You mean there's a Senator for all this?'"

Snyder often orients the reader with place names: "Sourdough Mountain at the hub of six valleys: Skagit, Thunder, Ruby, Upper Skagit, Pierce Creek and Stetattle Creek." I repeated the names like a mantra.

Snyder brought a calm and centered soul to the beats and the hippies. He also introduced a beat luminary to the crest. In *Earth House Hold* he recounts the time three hikers carrying fishing poles stared uncomprehendingly at an odd trio ambling up a trail near Kennedy Hot Springs: a young woman, an elfin figure with a goatee, and a bearded man with thick glasses and wild hair. The man with the beard spoke to the fishermen in a reassuring tone: "We are forest beatniks," he said.

The nonplused fishermen hustled down the trail, unaware that they had been addressed by Allen Ginsberg, in 1965 already acknowledged as the premier beat poet. Ginsberg, Snyder, and a female friend were en route to climb Glacier Peak the following day. It would be Ginsberg's first mountain.

He was an unlikely mountaineer. A layer of fat padded his frame, and he had spent his life in the city. From his childhood in Paterson, New

Jersey, he moved across the river to New York, where he threw himself into academia, a budding counterculture, and the nascent gay scene. He became a star at Columbia University, where he studied under the poet William Carlos Williams. As the bohemian center of gravity shifted west, he followed. By the time he started up Glacier Peak, he had written his best-known poem, *Howl*, as well as several volumes of verse for Lawrence Ferlinghetti's City Lights Books.

They set up high camp and read from the *100,000 Songs of Milarepa*, a Tibetan saint who lived on nettles at the base of Mount Everest. A predawn start gave them firm snow for the ascent. Ginsberg's perpetual cigarette glowed in the gloom. Before donning crampons, the party found sprawled at the glacier's edge the skeleton of a mountain goat, which seemed full of an unnameable significance. The sun found them negotiating the crevasses, and in due course they arrived at the summit. Snyder was elated. He told Ginsberg he had finally found the perfect climbing partner. Ginsberg felt honored and delighted, but he didn't become a mountaineer. He was a city boy to the bone. This most famous beat poet became the only one who failed to establish a deep relationship with the Cascades.

As far as the world was concerned, Jack Kerouac spoke for the Beat Generation. He ran rolls of newsprint paper through his typewriter in marathon writing sessions, knitting words, sentences, paragraphs across long arcs like Bird blowing his sax in a smoke-filled dream-drenched New York City joint, melodies punctuated with counter-rhythms, tonal asides, quotes, and searing cries, but always riding the beat.

Jack looked like the athlete he once was. Columbia offered him a football scholarship. His all-American good looks, soft voice, and high-speed prattle made a good first impression, but his heavy drinking and manic ways made him difficult company over the long haul. Rexroth admired Kerouac's literary gift, yet he despised his lack of discipline—probably because Kerouac shunned the labor of rewriting, which constitutes the definition of writing to craftsmen like Rexroth. Kerouac depended on his muse, taking dictation from his soul.

Snyder took Kerouac on a climb of 12,000-foot Matterhorn Peak in northern Yosemite National Park. He outfitted Kerouac at an Oakland surplus store and on the trip taught him the elements of camping. The hard-living Kerouac had a tough time keeping up with the Northwest woodsman but found the experience exalting. At Snyder's suggestion,

Right: *Afternoon light on the weathered Sourdough Lookout and the Snowfield Group.*

Kerouac resolved to work at a fire lookout in the North Cascades for the summer of 1956. The Forest Service assigned him to Desolation Peak, across the Skagit Valley from Sourdough.

On Desolation, Kerouac lived in perfect solitude and simplicity. The lookout had no electricity or plumbing. Not a single visitor crossed the threshold in the sixty-three days he spent on the summit. Besides the crackle of the radio, he heard only wind and thunder.

Years of life on the road had ground him down. Drugs, booze, false friends, hostile cops, and other tortures left him exhausted and despairing despite his huge appetite for life. Desolation Peak cleared his perception. He had the time to wrestle his demons to a draw, at least temporarily.

The grand scenery uplifted him. He later wrote that he fell in love with "Mount Hozomeen miles away by Canada leaning over my backyard and staring in my window." He listed the peaks and rivers, imbuing them with personalities and sensing an immanent spirituality. "I had a tremendous sensation of its dreamlikeness which never left me all that summer and in fact grew and grew."

His time on Desolation Peak became the climactic event in Kerouac's life. His experiences on the mountaintop became the source for the conclusion of *The Dharma Bums*, the opening chapters of *Desolation Angels*, verse for his collection *Book of Blues*, and the subject of an essay in *Lonesome Traveler*.

That summer was Kerouac's final reprieve. After writing about Desolation, his muse abandoned him. He failed to come to terms with fame and fell into alcoholism. He tried to put his life together one last

time in California's Big Sur, but he found the country spooky and soon returned to the city. He fled to his mother's house in Lowell, Massachusetts, instead of the mountains. Booze wrapped its tentacles tightly around him, and demons raged again. He withdrew from the world and died, bloated and empty at age forty-seven.

As I watched the last of the sun's rays light the little hut on Sourdough, I could imagine it when Gary Snyder lived there, Buddhist prayer flags rippling softly. Steel cables still held the square structure on the bedrock so storms wouldn't blow it over the cliff. Glaciers still caught the last light in basins to the south; the Pickets still cast long shadows over the ridges and valleys to the east. But I knew things were different now. The glaciers have receded perceptibly. The range now attracts scores of climbers and a cloud of hikers. Cars stream over State Route 20 where only a trail existed not long ago. Ginsberg, Kerouac, and Rexroth are dead. As Snyder is fond of pointing out, everything is impermanent: thoughts, lives, mountains, stars.

Left: *Night falling on the Sourdough Lookout, a lonely and cozy refuge.*

Ice: Snowfield to Inspiration

"We set up a

well-ventilated tent

and hid from our

flying tormentors."

CHAPTER

5

ice: snowfield to inspiration

The route to Snowfield Peak is nasty and brutish, but not short enough. Jim Nelson and I embarked on the Pyramid Lake trail late one July morning, the grade easy, the footpath well maintained, the packs onerous. We reeled in the trail, girdled the lake, and then followed a very direct and dusty climber's path on its trajectory toward a ridge below Pyramid Peak. Summer sun reached through the trees and I was drenched in sweat.

We stopped on a sunny hillock on the crest of the ridge. We would lose a few hundred feet and then ascend a steep bit before the ridge laid back on its final approach to the fields of snow. We stepped off the ridge and into a prototypical Cascade bush bash. Alder and other demon brush snagged my clothes and hung up on my pack. When the way shifted toward vertical, I grabbed roots and branches to make progress. No amount of hydration could keep up with the heat. To complete the experience, swarms of mosquitoes congregated and commenced feeding. I began to fantasize about helicopters with something akin to lust. After an eon, we topped the ridge again and staggered to camp. The mosquitoes thickened in the still air.

At least the view was grand. An energetic Colonial Creek danced in its canyon. To the north, we could see to the end of Ross Lake, and I fancied I could pick out the Sourdough Mountain lookout perched on its rocky prominence. Tomorrow's route ran up a snow ramp below Pyramid Peak. We set up a well-ventilated tent and hid from our flying tormentors.

We awoke to another fine day. The bugs reposed in a morning torpor as Jim and I hightailed it for the snow. We moved up quickly. Soon Pyramid and Paul Bunyan's Stump were insignificant bumps below us. We traversed firm snow to a pass below Snowfield Peak and climbed carefully to the top on loose, nontechnical ground that would still exact a high price for error. We settled onto the capacious summit and awaited good light. Excepting the summit register, we saw no sign that other people had passed this way before us.

The mountains accepted our offerings of blood, sweat, and 18,000 burnt calories. Once again we could see the North Cascades from end to end. The Pickets sawed the atmosphere to the north and the granite monoliths above Washington Pass shimmered in the dry air to the east. Southward, we reveled in our view of the peaks north of the Inspiration ice cap. The sight of the north walls of the Austera Towers seemed as rare as a view of the dark side of the moon. The pale towers stood like tombstones. Behind and above them rose Eldorado Peak and the mountains surrounding Cascade Pass. We photographed until the last light faded, and then watched the bright dust of the Milky Way brighten from our lofty aerie.

Next morning, we photographed from our sleeping bags in the cold of first light. Beyond the snowfield we had traversed, Baker and Shuksan glowed. The sun had melted patterns in the snow surface, which was

Right: *Icebergs from the Price Glacier congregate at the outlet of the lake.*

painted with orange algae. We packed and descended efficiently, retracing our two-day approach in eight hours, back to the heat of midsummer and the noisy bustle of life in the lowlands. The vision of the ice cap haunted my imagination.

One year later my friend Cathy Kraus sat on her pack in the snow of Inspiration Glacier and coiled the rope absently. She was reeling me in for a snack and a rest. I felt discouraged by her peppy demeanor. Cathy runs marathons, lifts weights, and looks it. I had done my best to cloak my undignified gasping on our climb as she talked easily, commenting on the marvels our route revealed. Now I could see our projected camp on a pass at the base of Klawatti Peak and looked forward to respite from our day of crossing the ice.

Klawatti is on the axis of the iciest region of the North Cascades crest. You can wander on ice almost all the way from Park Creek Pass west of Stehekin to the gap between Newhalem and McAllister Creeks east of Marblemount. The Inspiration, Klawatti, and McAllister Glaciers cohere to create the largest ice cap in the range. The Boston Glacier hugs the north side of nearby Forbidden and Boston Peaks. Small unnamed glaciers have staked out territories north and south. From Klawatti, you can see it all.

You can hear it, too. The ice groans and cracks under your feet. Where glacier ice flows over cliffs, towers of ice known as seracs topple with a crash and disintegrate, sometimes triggering snow avalanches or scattering chunks of ice the size of sedans. In the valley, meltwater roars off cliffs or tears through soft moraines.

The Tepeh Towers (*tepeh* is a native word meaning "quills") punch through the ice field like knuckles. Geologists call small peaks surrounded by glacial ice nunataks, also a native word. Klawatti is the largest of the nunataks here. This landscape resembles the interior of icy Baffin Island or the edge of the Antarctic plateau. It is an ice desert—a desert fed by blizzards instead of sandstorms.

In early season, few crevasses are in view high in the accumulation zone, the engine of the glacier. The remnants of recent winters, layered under fresh snow, compress into glacial ice. If accumulation from years past is sufficient, the glacier advances, pushing rock and soil forward like a bulldozer. If snowfall has been sparse, the glacier retreats, leaving scoured rock in its wake. In either case, in full years or lean, the reaction of the glacier to accumulation is delayed for years. The weight of the accumulation forces the glacier downhill just inches per day.

Geologists guess that twenty ice ages sculpted the North Cascades in the past 2.5 million years. They have to guess because later glaciers obliterated evidence of earlier episodes. Continental glaciers came down from the north, and alpine glaciers followed valleys once sluiced by rivers. In the heyday of Pleistocene glaciation during the last million years, all the North Cascade mountains were either submerged in ice or peeked above it as isolated nunataks.

Fifteen thousand years ago at the height of the last glaciation period, the Cordilleran ice sheet almost buried the North Cascades crest. It had swept south from British Columbia, which it covered entirely. Where modern pocket glaciers now fight a losing battle against melting, rivers

Left: *Crevasses curve over the surface of the Boston Glacier like brushstrokes.*

Following page: *Mount Baker's Coleman Glacier tumbles in slow motion over a steep wall.*

of ice thousands of feet thick flowed out of the mountains onto the plains to merge with this great ice sheet, which was flensing the forests and excavating a deeper Puget Sound.

In historic times ice has rapidly advanced and retreated in mini ice ages. As recently as the late nineteenth century, the glaciers pulsed forward. The loose end (terminal) moraines in evidence today date from those times. Glaciers now are retreating at an astonishing rate. Of 756 North Cascade glaciers identified in a 1969 inventory, 17 have now shrunk to where they no longer meet the definition of a glacier: moving ice covering at least one-tenth of a square kilometer.

Today, many pocket glaciers still grind in small basins they scooped out over millennia. When glaciers from adjacent basins almost come together, they sculpt knife-edge ridges. Often the hardest rock survives as monolithic towers that appear fragile, but are adamantine at their core.

Glaciers transport mountains to the sea with water. Meltwater loaded with the ground-up rock particles known as glacial flour streams from the tongues of glaciers. The fine particles remain suspended in the fast-moving water, coloring it gray or brown. But in the still waters of a lake, the flour transforms the color to turquoise, aquamarine, or emerald.

While ice displays its power most dramatically in glaciers, it wreaks almost as much change on the landscape working covertly. Every talus slope testifies to the action of frost and ice. Water freezes in cracks and faults in the rock. As the water freezes into ice and expands, it pries blocks apart and, in geologic time, tosses them down the slope.

At the end of our day on the ice cap, Cathy and I put up the tent even though we saw no threat in the sky. Balancing the stove on some talus, we cooked dinner. For a while we ignored the magnificence and tried to concentrate on our humdrum tasks, but the mountains tugged at our attention.

Inspiration Glacier chilled the wind. Melting slowed. Snow hardened. Minutes after sunset the sky began to blaze with the sun's dying light. Mountains glowed like molten rock and clouds resembled flames, but it was a momentary incandescence. The clouds soon grayed, and indigo chased the glow from the sky and obscured the peaks while the cold sent us to our sleeping bags.

The crisp, clear morning presaged a day of baking heat. We started at first light so we could walk on hard snow before the sun reduced it to the consistency of a snow cone. Traversing the glacier parallel to the crevasses added to the hazard, but it was unavoidable for getting where we needed to go.

Crevasses tend to form perpendicular to the direction the glacier is moving. When you cross a crevasse field while climbing or descending the glacier, you intersect the crevasses instead of traveling alongside them. Then, if you fall into a crevasse, your partner on the rope can usually stop the fall. But when moving parallel to a crevasse as Cathy and I were doing, both climbers can fall into it simultaneously. We took extra care.

By late morning we had veered toward Eldorado Peak. The route steepened and narrowed to a small-scale version of an Alaskan ridge, minus the double cornices. From the snow-dome summit of Eldorado, the icy terrain was laid out like an aerial photograph. To the southeast, Cascade Pass appeared as a low notch. Sheer cliffs encircled the Marble Creek cirque to the west; we gazed upon miles of granitic faces, steep snow tongues, airy buttresses.

We declared victory and began the long descent to the head of Eldorado Creek, girding ourselves for hours of talus hopping and shin-killing forest path. While focused on my footing, I missed the exit from a boulder field, wasting fifteen minutes I had intended to dedicate to lolling in the car. With the path relocated, the rest of the descent went without a hitch, finding the tree-crossing of the Cascade River.

My feet hurt, but Cathy was still full of energy. She volunteered to jog back to the car while I guarded the packs. I couldn't muster the weakest protest. As she sprang up the gravel road like an impala, I resolved henceforth to always hike with runners.

Cascade Pass: The Triplets in Winter

"Jim leaned around the

bulge and sunk his ax into thick

ice with a satisfying thunk."

| CHAPTER |

cascade pass: the triplets in winter

Winter climbing in the Cascades makes little sense. Wet-snow avalanches set like poured concrete, cloud cover masks approaching storms, and arctic winds shiver the peaks. Melting snow and occasional rain soak equipment. An honest memory of a winter climb is a litany of miseries.

In the warmth of the living room, our plans had the ring of sweet reason. Jim Nelson, one of the region's best winter climbers, proposed an unclimbed line on the north wall of Johannesburg Mountain. If that ice climb proved too ambitious, we would scamper up a short gully on the neighboring Triplets.

As our car nosed up the snow-covered Cascade River Road, conditions seemed perfect: high clouds, cool temperatures, old avalanche debris at the base of the steep gullies called couloirs. Our intended route came into view after a mile of snowshoeing. The early-season ice hadn't yet filled the couloir on Johannesburg as we had hoped it would, so instead we trudged up to Cascade Pass, intent on bagging the Triplets. We dug a snow trench for shelter against the building wind, which soon shooed us into our bivouac sacks. We carried no tent; we knew that going fast meant going light. But I regretted not bringing one, as spindrift sneaked into my bivy sack and my sleeping bag. At least I had brought a sleeping bag. Jim had opted for only a half bag zipped to a down jacket.

A cloudless sky greeted us in the morning. After the usual winter struggle with clothing and breakfast, we slowly hiked to the Triplets.

The peak looks like the back of a hand with fingers extended. In winter, thin runnels of ice and snow clog the lines between the fingers. We decided to try the left-hand runnel. Despite being surrounded by higher peaks, the Triplets commanded respect. Snow plumed from the summits and tortuous gullies hid the difficulties. We donned crampons and roped up at the base, and started ascending together.

Almost immediately, thin ice slowed us. I still expected, however, to summit near midday. The fact that we had left our headlamps and bivy gear in camp didn't trouble me. We were light and fast.

The ice disappeared entirely, leaving a leftward traverse across bare rock toward the narrowing gully. To my relief Jim gathered the gear and led. His crampon points ground against stone as he placed them on tiny edges. Compact rock rejected pitons. After much fussing, he hammered in two thin pitons thirty feet up, which we recognized as psychological protection. They likely wouldn't hold a fall.

As he stepped around a bulge, he called down: "Watch me. I'm terrified." This was not welcome news. Jim normally relished climbs that drove me to consider confining my thrill-seeking to chess matches and wedding photography. Any bit of climbing that slowed him at all would be desperate business for me.

Jim leaned around the bulge and sank his ax into thick ice with a satisfying thunk. After surmounting twenty feet of what appeared to be vertical ice, he called for me to follow.

I felt the reassuring tug of the rope as I moved quickly to the two pitons. I whacked at the pitons with my hammer, trying to do my job of removing them. The bulge forced my body away from the ice, and my pack threatened to pull me off. Jim's intermittent tugs pulled me sideways. If I lost my grip, I would swing across the traverse and slam into a wall, away from climbable rock. The pitons finally popped out, and I swung around the bulge with more desperation than elegance. Panting against the ice, I paused to wonder why I kept coming back to winter climbing. Bad memory, I concluded.

Right: *Jim Nelson speeding up easy ground low on the Triplets.*

On closer inspection the sheet of vertical ice became a cluster of detached icicles. To ascend, one foot clawed the hanging ice while the other sought purchase on wet rock between the icicles. It was all coming back to me. The tug on the rope became a pull as Jim winched me up.

Midday was already a memory, but the route eased back and our optimism returned. The gully necked down to six feet across and zigzagged up, obscuring the route, but the loose snow allowed us to create steps and move quickly. With luck, we could still get up and off before dark. Growing urgency propelled us upward. As we ascended, the snow deepened and softened, slowing us and reducing security. We surmounted a couple difficult steps before arriving at the funnel of a small snow bowl. Jim laboriously packed the powder into steps and swam to the top of the gully as evening alpenglow tinted the surrounding peaks. It was late. We were in trouble.

We retraced our steps downward, racing the light. The deep snow and narrow gully passed quickly, but the technical steps stopped us. We needed anchors to fix the rope so we could rappel down. But the ice was too thin for ice screws and the rock lacked cracks for pitons. In the gathering gloom Jim hacked a channel in a three-inch-thick patch of ice adhering to a boulder, draped a sling in the channel, and hung the rope from the sling. It held. After passing that obstacle, he hammered a piton into a bottoming crack, attached the rope, and slid down to easier ground. Night extinguished the last glow on the horizon.

The worst was over, but the moonless night yielded little light. We picked our way down unroped, unable to see our feet. The slope steepened. A section that seemed trivial in daylight required perfect placements. The terrain dipped to 60 degrees. Crampon points and axes bounced off rock behind thin ice. Concentration battled with haste and fatigue. I forced myself to focus all attention on each placement. The world became very small and compelling.

I found Jim inspecting every square inch of a ledge at the base of this section. We were atop a fifty-foot cliff, though just below I could see a gentle slope dipping to Cascade Pass. The expanse of snow reflected starlight, and the glow of nearby towns silhouetted the peaks. No wind interrupted a perfect silence.

"No anchors," Jim announced.

While I would have preferred a miracle, I resigned myself to a night of doing jumping jacks to stay warm. We had survived. We would get off

Left: *In winter the great walls of the Northern Pickets look Alaskan in character.*

the ledge at first light, with all body parts intact.

"I've got something," Jim said.

He had found a hole in the rock by fumbling blindly. He threaded a sling through the hole. After a minute of aggressive testing, we rappelled down to our snowshoes. An hour later we found our snow trench and wiggled into frozen bivouac sacks.

Next morning the wind wailed across the pass, blowing snow hundreds of feet into space. We hurried to the car with the wind pummeling our backs. The North Cascades had spit us out.

Left: *Because a shovel weighs less than a tent, we slept in a trench.*

Right: *Mount Slesse has some of the longest technical routes in the North Cascades.*

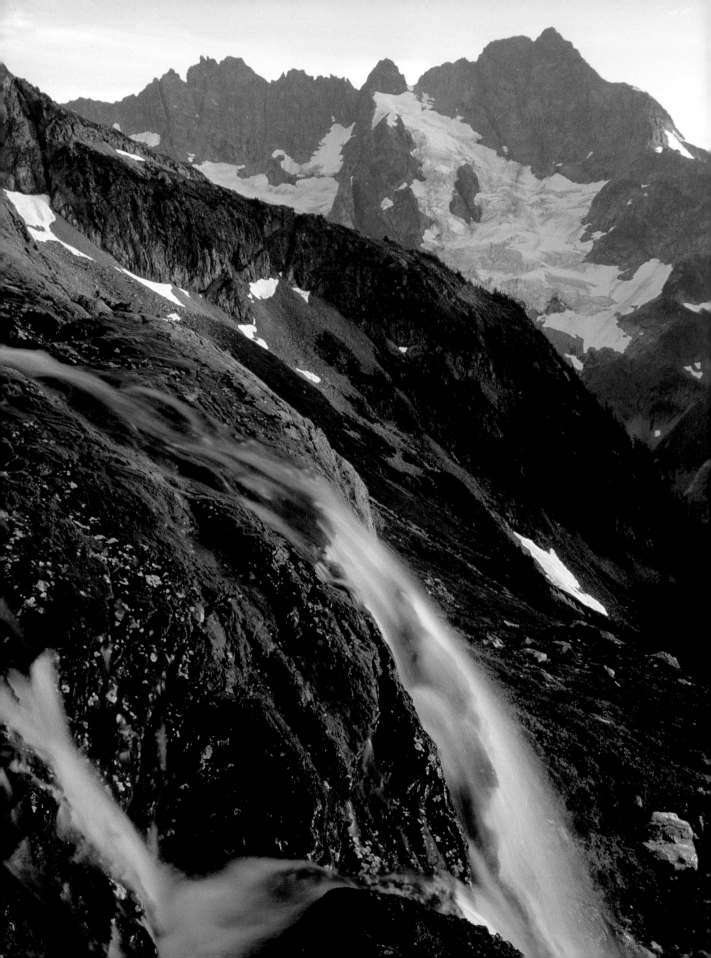

Ptarmigan: Life on the Crest

"We roamed

through heather

gardens. . . ."

CHAPTER

7

ptarmigan: life on the crest

The Ptarmigan Traverse spurned me on my first attempt. My wife, Terrie, and I decided to give the famous high route a try. We thought the short, cool days of mid-September would have swept the crowds out of the mountains. We were correct, but the crowds apparently used better judgment than we did.

We planned to travel light. We reverted to a plastic tube tent, hoping for fair skies and reasoning that it would work in a pinch. We would carry five days' worth of food, and simply go hungry if pinned by weather.

We left Seattle late and rumbled up the Cascade River Road after lunch. The interminable switchbacks of the Cascade Pass trail consumed a couple hours. We broke out of the forest under gray skies. Pikas whistled with irritation as we passed their talus-slope home on the long traverse to the pass. We trudged up Mixup Arm, balanced carefully on the loose moraines hanging between cliffs east of the arm, and ascended the small glacier below the narrow high-mountain pass known as Cache Col as the late summer sun set. We camped on the col and enjoyed our circumscribed view between Magic and Mixup Peaks.

The Ptarmigan Traverse got its name from the Ptarmigan Climbing Club, in turn named for that high-country grouse; don't pronounce the "p"). In 1938 four members bushwhacked from Sulphur Creek to Dome Peak and pioneered the route between Dome and Cascade Pass that bears the club's name. After reaching the pass, they climbed Sahale, Boston, and Buckner Peaks—all in one day. They returned to their car at Sulphur Creek via Agnes Creek and Suiattle Pass after thirteen days out. The traverse wasn't repeated for fifteen years.

Tom Miller's photographs in *The North Cascades* (published by The Mountaineers, 1964) document the second success on the traverse in 1953. I remembered a shot from Cache Col where we now sat—a black-and-white photo of three crew-cut young men sorting food in the morning sun, boxes of Jell-O, Grape Nuts, and Minute Rice, with the washed-out image of Formidable Glacier looming behind them. From the cloistered gloom of my high school library, these young men seemed like gods, American versions of legendary alpinists Bonatti and Buhl. I prayed I would someday have the fortitude to follow in their footsteps.

It was now thirty-five years since Miller took the photo, and I didn't like the look of the moody gray clouds that hovered over us while we hopped down a talus slope to Kool Aid Lake. The so-called lake proved to be little more than a puddle. (Legend has it that a group of thirsty Mountaineers poured all their Kool Aid mix into the tarn, turning it into a giant beverage.)

The terrain from the tarn to Formidable Glacier was archetypal Cascade cruising. We roamed through heather gardens, miniature green groves stripped of their ornaments. Mossy brooks meandered over benches, lingering a moment before hurtling over cliffs to the valley below. Behind us, the backside of Johannesburg Mountain hunched huge and dark. Ahead, the aptly named Mount Formidable lay in waiting.

Late-season ice necessitated crampons on the glacier, but the crevasses were open and easy to avoid. Our immediate goal, the col between Spider and Formidable Peaks, came into view in early afternoon. All we could hear in the windless silence was the crunch of our boots.

Our first view south from the col was a shock. A wall of blue-gray cloud was speeding toward us like a tidal wave, and a gale-force wind rammed into us. Terrie threw down her pack and pulled out her rain gear. I did the same, zipping the shell closed just as the monsoon blew in. It felt like stepping into a cold shower. We had to shout to hear each other over the wind howl. We scurried down an icy gully on the south side as fast as safety would permit.

The storm settled into a steady rain as we traversed to Yang Yang Lakes. We found a site on high ground and set up the tube tent, a sorry shelter in a real downpour. Memories of drowned camps past came unbidden to mind. We battened down the tent, but wind-borne rain sneaked under the roof while rivulets broached the artificial dams we constructed, creating pools that chased us and soaked our bags despite our contortions. By morning we were ready to flee. We retraced two days of hiking in one long day, dogged by mist every step of the way.

Years earlier Jim Nelson and I blitzkrieged the southern end of the Ptarmigan Traverse during a Northwest heat wave. Traveling as light as possible, we sped up Downey Creek, clambered over the deadfall and bashed through the sweltering brush of Bachelor Creek, continued over an unnamed pass, and descended to Itswoot Lake where we paused for dinner. We luxuriated for half an hour before heading out again across verdant hillsides and up steep tongues of soft snow. Near sunset we unshouldered our packs on the crest of Itswoot Ridge and crawled into our bags. A dusky full moon rose east of Glacier Peak. The last of the sun bathed its Fuji-perfect slopes in salmon and coral tints. After dark we contemplated the moon's frozen geology.

You can't carry a truly light pack on a multiday climbing trip, but Jim had pared equipment to a minimum. We carried only one rope instead of two, saving a lot of weight—but also halving the distance we could descend with each rappel. This could prove inconvenient or even dangerous. Our rack of gear for climbing protection was anorexic: a few

camming devices and a handful of chocks. In the place of more hardware we carried extra fabric slings to hook over rock horns and between
big blocks. A tent fly took the place of a tent; we could use our ice axes
for poles and wait out a blow in safety if not comfort. Instead of using
our stove to melt snow for drinking water, we saved on fuel by filling
dark-colored stuff sacks with snow and letting it slowly liquefy on its
own. All the food was instant, requiring no simmering. Each little trick
saved pounds and contributed to our ability to move fast.

We were up at first light to take advantage of firm snow. After some
sidehilling, we stared up the west side of Dome Peak from Dome Glacier.
The snow slope gradually steepened. Jim raced ahead, the rope still in
his pack. While the terrain wasn't too difficult, I hadn't been on snow
for a while, so I paid close attention to the placement of my feet and the
ice ax. I balanced using the tip of the ax shaft until the slope tilted near

the top, forcing use of the pick. From here, a blocky ridge that ran north to the main peak also tended south to our goal, a subsidiary horn, the southwest peak.

Jim was already tied in to his harness, the rope neatly flaked out, the gear rack slung under one arm. I settled into position to give him a protective belay and he took off. I could barely play out the rope fast enough. Minutes later, I broke down the belay and followed. The climbing was easy but airy and athletic. I could swing like a gibbon on the big holds, moving quickly and freely without the burden of a big rack. I removed the pieces of protection Jim had placed for himself and joined him in 150 feet. I grabbed the remainder of the light rack and led to the summit. I barely had time to look around before Jim joined me. We found a register and were surprised to learn we were just the eleventh party to climb the southwest peak.

Two hours later we were on the main summit of Dome, eating lunch and trying to identify the myriad peaks. The immediate neighborhood looked prime for climbing. Instead of the usual metamorphic rubble, the rock here came from a granitic outcrop. Straight, even cracks split the steepest faces. Jim envisioned new routes for the sheer walls of Dome's easterly neighbor, Gunsight Peak. An easy descent on sloppy snow brought us back to our packs. The sun had reddened our skin and parched our throats. We camped on an island of rock adjacent to Dome Glacier and devoted the rest of the day to rest and rehydration.

After a cold breakfast the next morning, we crossed a shoulder of Dome to reach Dana Glacier and then descended to the base of Elephant's Head, a distinctive scooped horn. Two elegant ridges bracket its north face. We put on our rock shoes and scrambled to the start of the unclimbed northwest ridge. The first pitch was the crux. Jim led up a near-vertical grainy crack. On first ascents, grit and grunge still adhere to the rock. Jim passed a slight overhang and established a bombproof belay, giving me the confidence to follow with enthusiasm and grace. Then it was my turn to set out on the sharp end of the rope to lead the next pitch. I was relieved to find moderate climbing. At one point, though, I pulled up on a stubby horn that broke off in my hand. I barn-doored into space, hinged to the rock on one jammed foot and a jammed hand. The horn whistled past Jim, who looked up in some irritation. He wore no helmet—we had left them home to save weight.

Thereafter the angle slackened. We made the top in short order,

Previous page: *Sunset at Kool Aid Lake under the walls of Mount Johannesburg.*

Left: *In winter crowds of bald eagles patrol the Skagit River in search of fish.*

tarrying for a while to study Gunsight from a new angle. Then it was the usual descent—blocky down-climbing, sandy ledges, muddy steps, and some steep snow that we had to negotiate in our slick-soled rock shoes.

The sun had gone from bake to broil. We hustled back to camp, broke it down, and began a death march across slushy snow to Itswoot Ridge. We were on our way home. We hurried back to the lake and then up the pass. We hoped to reach Downey Creek by dark. It was not to be: We gave up in the tall timber past Bachelor Creek's brush, lying down in the middle of the trail. Three hours of hiking the next morning returned us to the car and back to the city's heat.

Several years later, I returned to the Ptarmigan Traverse with Himalayan expedition leader Jim Frush and his friend Kristin Day. I had just come down from Klawatti Peak, north of Cascade Pass. I caught a shower and a night in bed, and then rendezvoused with Jim and Kristin on the east side of Cascade Pass the following afternoon. Frowsy deer loitered near camp. Next morning, we discovered they had eaten the sweat-soaked T-shirts we had hung to dry overnight. Mourning our loss, we hiked over Cache Col to Kool Aid Lake and camped on a grassy island in the rocks.

Snow still ringed the tarn in mid-August. Thin clouds muted the afternoon light. Jim and Kristin had an early dinner and retired as the sun set over Johannesburg. I prowled the area alone searching for good photographic compositions. The last light illuminated the outlet creek waterfall, so I shot a few frames with Mount Formidable in the background. When the light faded I sat on a boulder to watch the sky go dark. Drab light smothered hope for a good sunset.

But then, slowly, the clouds warmed. The sun was over the horizon yet it spun a tapestry of reds, yellows, and oranges. I planted my chin on snow at the water's edge and saw a mirror of the show in the sky. I shot as quickly as I could, first toward Johannesburg and the Triplets and then, as the light cooled, south toward Formidable. When the light finally failed, I packed up and returned to camp where Jim and Kristin slept unaware of the show they missed.

The next morning I awoke to snuffling noises and the sound of ripping grass. I unzipped the tent door, and half a dozen scrawny deer peered inside. They had strayed above their range. I surmised that food

Right: *Marmot sentries warn their neighbors when intruders approach.*

was scarce down in the forest, probably from overpopulation caused by the peak of a boom-and-bust cycle.

Deer so high were new to me. Transient black bears sometimes visit en route to adjacent valleys, but usually rodents—pikas, marmots, and mice—are the largest mammals I've seen above tree line.

Hoary marmots favor the high country. They lounge on boulders on sunny days and feign unconcern when hikers pass, but they maintain a vigilant watch for predators, signaling danger with a distinctive whistle. If roused to action, they gallop on stubby legs like furry sumo wrestlers. These chubby critters are the largest members of the squirrel family, growing to two feet in length. They must pack on the pounds in the

short alpine summer for their winter hibernation, yet they go about their business with the deliberation of bears. When the days shorten and temperatures drop, they decamp to their dens, beginning hibernation before the snow falls. Respiration and heartbeat slow, body temperature drops, and other bodily systems arrest until spring awakens them.

Pikas act more concerned than marmots. They quickly bark, bleat, or whistle a warning to their kin when catching sight of humans or other potential threats. They keep to the rock piles where good lookouts and easy getaways abound. They rarely venture more than fifty to a hundred feet from their burrows. Some folks call them rock rabbits (early explorers identified them as a type of tiny hare), but they don't hop and their ears are round like small radar dishes, not elongated like a bunny's. Pikas are models of industry. One rarely appears without carrying tufts of grass

in its mouth to prepare a den for the long winter. Unlike marmots, pikas don't hibernate and so require food stores instead of fat.

Marmots are the pikas' unwitting allies. The call of a distressed marmot sends pikas scurrying for cover. Martens, coyotes, foxes, and bobcats commute to the North Cascades crest in search of both marmots and pikas. Eagles and hawks patrol for the high-altitude rodents, too. When marmots retire for the winter, pikas invade the vacated territory to forage for their winter stocks. They harvest dried marmot droppings, presumably for the undigested plant material it contains.

While marmots and pikas are common, the dread snafflehounds are ubiquitous. Also known as pack rats, these bushy-tailed rodents invade the most unlikely sites. Even on hard-won bivouac ledges, snafflehounds ransack packs and food stores of incautious climbers, making off with items to add to their nests. They like shiny objects: bits of foil, utensils, climbing hardware. It's always prudent to hang your gear beyond their reach in pack-rat country, which is everywhere in the North Cascades.

White-tailed ptarmigan are the largest animals to live above tree line year-round. In the summer months, they putter about, shepherding their broods and foraging for food. They depend on camouflage to protect themselves from predators, especially hawks. When hikers encounter them, these diminutive grouse cousins scurry away conspicuously to draw attention from their young. Ptarmigan avoid the summer snow patches, but come winter, their feathers turn pure white. They dig into the snow to look for willow sprigs to eat, safe in their new camouflage.

Most animal life on the crest is smaller in scale. In midsummer everyone contends with mosquitoes. At their peak they swarm in Alaskan numbers, puncturing skin and raising bumps, clogging nostrils, and whining incessantly while seeming to darken the sky. Fortunately, these flying hypodermic needles don't carry disease in the Cascades.

There's nothing exotic about horseflies. These domestic annoyances arrive when the mosquito population dwindles in the interval between snowmelt and the first chill of fall. They bite tiny chunks of flesh from unprotected arms and legs, drawing blood and curses. A slap doesn't deter them. The trick is to stun them, then crush them underfoot with a satisfying crunch.

Below the crest, mosquito territory and boggy travel is signified by blooming monkey flower, the evocative elephant's head, tiger lilies, and especially shooting stars. In the dark of dry forests, parasitic, fleshy

Left: *Penstemon prefer rocky terrain or dry open spaces.*

plants such as pine drops and candystick thrive without chlorophyll, feeding on fungi. At times mushrooms abound. The amanita mushrooms are beautiful but can cause hallucinations, nausea, even death, if eaten. Mushroom gourmets prize chanterelles, oysters, angel's wings, and the admirable boletus.

Plants on the crest lie low to withstand its harsh conditions. They reproduce quickly in the brief interval between snowmelt and the rebuilding of the snowpack in October. Avalanche lilies appear first, carpeting alpine meadows in white. When the flowers peak, one can see penstemon, pussytoes, phlox, lupine, columbine, paintbrush, saxifrage, and cinquefoil as well as the heathers in one day of hiking near tree line. The silent white bells of Cassiope were John Muir's favorite alpine flower.

Some of the most beautiful flowers stake out territories above tree line. Mats of red-stemmed, white-petaled alpine saxifrage hug sandy soil while moss campion and spreading phlox mass in aerodynamic convex colonies to withstand fierce winds. Silky phacelia confronts the elements, standing tall with a ball of numerous purple petals and a pincushion of thin gold-tipped pistils atop a sturdy violet stem. It favors rocky nooks that afford some protection from wind and rain.

Here the pines are twisted and stunted, the junipers huddle against the wind. Lichens decorate stone with a broad palette of colors. They create irregular geometric patterns or concentrate in undifferentiated mats. Lichens eat through solid rock, eroding the range a molecule at a time. Red algae seem to carpet the snow late in the year.

From my vantage point on Kool Aid Lake, I can see dark forest on either side of the Middle Fork of the Cascade River far below. Species of cedar and hemlock stand shoulder to shoulder from river's edge to tree line at about 5,000 feet. Red alder, vine maple, salmonberry, and black cottonwood choke avalanche chutes that scar the forest.

Although the North Cascades crest appears pristine and protected, it is under subtle attack, most notably by those who love it. Deep ruts furrow the heather benches on the Ptarmigan Traverse from a relatively small number of hikers each year, and the unmaintained approach paths suffer from erosion. We foul the water and spook the wildlife.

The worst depredations occur outside protected areas. Congress drew the boundaries of North Cascades National Park and neighboring wilderness areas based more on economics and political exigencies than science, so the ecosystem frays at the edges. A patchwork of clear-cut

Right: *The secretive lynx is seldom seen.*

logging areas abuts the boundaries, triggering erosion and the silting of streams, which in turn causes the diminution or loss of salmon and steelhead stocks and the animals that depend on them. Timber companies replant logged areas with only a few species, destroying biodiversity. Smog drifts in from Seattle and Vancouver with undocumented effects. The federal government has identified numerous species that have dwindled or disappeared since white settlers first arrived. Bald eagles, peregrine falcons, owls, and northern goshawks are rare or threatened.

Grizzly bears were largely chased out of the North Cascades, but conservationists argue it is time to bring them back. Opponents argue that the bears are too dangerous—but safe and sanitized wilderness loses its value. Experienced wilderness travelers understand that danger is both inevitable and necessary. The mountains are the bears' home; we are just visitors. We must adapt and will be the richer for it.

Other large species maintain a foothold in the range. A few gray wolves have ventured back, while the fate of wolverines, lynx, and moose remains unclear. It may be too late to arrest the impoverishment of the North Cascades biosphere.

Back on the Ptarmigan Traverse, Jim and Kristin and I climbed over the Spider-Formidable col under a gray blanket of cloud. We had two tents and plenty of food, so I didn't worry about a repeat of my earlier fiasco on the traverse. As we hiked, the sun poked through the fluffy cumulus. We stopped early to enjoy Yang Yang Lakes, puttering around, taking shelter when showers raked the area and exploring during the dry intervals. No other parties disturbed our solitude.

The sun came out in earnest the next morning. We followed a steep dirt path to a bench south of the lakes and traversed to Le Conte Glacier and the pass leading to the South Cascade Glacier. We had stepped into an empty quarter of the range. Only traversers visit the stretch between Yang Yang and White Rock Lakes. Old Guard Peak, wrapped in Le Conte Glacier, looked down upon us, and we could hear Flat Creek far below.

The sun softened the snow. We moved softly over the glacier, taking care to find the thickest bridges over the crevasses and knocking away snow that balled under our crampons so that we wouldn't slip. We lost

Right: *Black bears spend most of their time in the forest below the crest.*

Following page: *The Dana Glacier spills into the Agnes Creek valley, as seen from White Rock Lakes camp.*

the route to the South Cascade Glacier. We elected to go straight down from the pass, which was a mistake. We squandered an hour on intricate down-climbing and rappels. After gaining the glacier, we toiled to the next pass, the one leading to White Rock Lakes. The rock and snow reflected the sun like an oven. Glare and fatigue sapped us with not even a zephyr to moderate the heat.

I perked up at the pass. A fresh breeze blew up from the Agnes Creek valley, countering the heat reflecting from the glacier. We were treated to a new view as well, a familiar landscape from a fresh perspective.

After admiring the line on Elephant's Head that Jim Nelson and I had climbed, we slid down the couloir to White Rock Lakes. The lakes are set at the back of a huge amphitheater. Spire Point, Dome Peak, and

the crevasse-riven Chickamin Glacier presented a menacing barrier to travel. We knew the route home passed near Spire's summit, but ridges obstructed our view of the route.

Rain accompanied the dawn. We waited in the tents all day. The next day we awoke to clouds, but broke camp anyway. Blind routefinding on misty glacier took us to the right pass next to Spire. We followed the easiest route down the rubbly south side of Spire and found two of our friends camped on Itswoot Ridge. After tea we sped down out of the wet all the way to Downey Creek. Dark caught us with miles to go, but stubbornness and the vision of cold beer drove us on. Headlamps added almost enough light for safe travel.

With two miles to go I felt my ankle roll, accompanied by a loud snap. It was 11 P.M. We stashed my pack, to be retrieved later. I hobbled deliberately and painfully for hours, leaning on two ice axes for support. I feared my ankle would swell and freeze up if we stopped. Finally we reached the road, and we drove quickly off to attend to our first priority. We pulled into an all-night convenience store in Darrington at 3 A.M. Unlike justice, beer delayed is not beer denied.

The emergency room doctor informed me that I'd suffered a serious sprain, not a break. I lost a week to crutches, and pain kept me citybound for a few weeks more, but the cost of experiencing the Ptarmigan Traverse was a bargain, to my way of thinking.

Right: *Mist swirls around the summit of Elephant's Head, a spur of Dome Peak.*

Glacier Peak: Terminus

"The low sun lit Glacier's

western flanks, bathing the snow

and ice with pale pink tints. . . ."

CHAPTER

glacier peak: terminus

Suiattle was still in flood on July 17. The river looked like liquid dust churning over boulders and down cascades. The trail to Image Lake on Miner's Ridge followed the river for nine miles, gaining only 1,000 feet of elevation before soaring uphill for 3,000 feet on six miles of low-angle switchbacks baking on a south-facing slope. Topping out on Miner's Ridge left a mellow mile to camp. It was going to be a tough day.

After driving to the end of the Suiattle road a few miles past the Downey Creek portal to the Ptarmigan Traverse, I enjoyed hiking in the

cool of the dark cedar and fir forest. At first, ferns and devil's club dominated the understory; sometimes moss carpeted the forest floor, draping over soil, rock, and fallen trees. Parasitic candystick plants stood in rows. The forest creaked in the breeze and I heard the machine-gun echo of woodpeckers at work. Small mice scurried at the edge of my vision. Rising less than one hundred feet per mile, the trail felt almost level.

At 2,900 feet its character changed to a relentless series of switchbacks zigzagging first through thinning trees and then over open county. The final mile to Image Lake clove close to the crest of Miner's Ridge. I could see Spire and Gunsight, two of the southernmost peaks of the Ptarmigan Traverse, over the rocky ridge of the Bath Lake high route, a rugged alternative approach to Miner's Ridge. To the south, the perfect cone of Glacier Peak dominated the skyline, dwarfing all other mountains, the last great eminence before Rainier.

The ridge was clad in short grasses, low blueberry, and a garland of wildflowers: lupine, tiger lily, columbine, and sweet valerian. Open meadows and sparse forest run east-west for miles and curve around Glacier Peak. The floor of the upper Suiattle River valley looks like the tree-covered terminus of an Alaskan glacier. Geologists call this the Great Fill, because over millennia, floods and stream erosion deposited sand and gravel. Relatively recent eruptions covered the Fill with a layer of pumice. Chocolate Creek and the Suiattle River carved deep grooves through the Fill.

I arrived at Image Lake by midafternoon. It nestled in a symmetrical green basin, catching the color of the sky and the mountain from one side while glowing emerald from the other. It was perfect beauty.

A friend once told me that I had no rational basis for my defense of wilderness—that at heart all my arguments were aesthetic. Guilty. I don't understand people with a blind spot for natural beauty, who miss the grandeur and bedrock strangeness of the non-human earth. I don't understand the allure of teeming cities where millions subsist cut off so much of the time from earth, sky, and fresh air. I don't know why anyone would want to live in a world without orangutans and grizzlies, lemurs and hammerhead sharks, without limitless vistas of untrammeled land.

Some folks argue for preservation by saying that otherwise we may destroy plants or animals that could aid people in some way. But I'm impatient with the utilitarian defense of wilderness. I don't see how humans, recent arrivals to this planet, can value all things only in

Left: *Glacier Peak and Image Lake, a study in symmetry.*

Following page: *Ridges ring Glacier Peak's cone. The tree-covered Great Fill is the remains of an ancient mudslide.*

proportion to how they may benefit our single rapacious species. True, the bark of the yew yields the anti-cancer agent taxol, and the secretions of certain frogs may prove to be safe and potent painkillers, and a host of cures and palliatives may await discovery, but all this misses the point. The natural world deserves respect for its own sake.

I left my pack by the lake and went to explore the ridge. From the ridge I dropped down past the abandoned Glacier Peak Mines, where the rock is shot through with copper ore, gaudy blue-and-green chrysocolla, and malachite. Some creeks here run over a bed of cool-hued, water-smoothed copper "eggs." But the copper is a curse on the wilderness. The world's insatiable markets hunger for more, and despoilers of the land are eager to accommodate them.

I'm amazed anyone would want to place an open-pit mine in the Glacier Peak Wilderness, but that is just what Kennecott Copper envisioned for the southern slope of Miner's Ridge. It was a nightmare scenario: Bulldozers, trucks, dynamite, and drills conspiring to scoop a half-mile-wide chunk out of the basin east of Image Lake, leaving only scars and the memory of a once wild place. The former mining village of Holden, one day's hike east of Image Lake, illustrates what we could expect if the mineral extractors got their way: toxic tailings, ruined streams, and savaged earth.

I give thanks to the Mountaineers, to the Mazamas, to David Brower and the Sierra Club, and to all the other conservationists who thwarted Kennecott's plans. But in the defense of wilderness, every victory is provisional and temporary.

My forebodings evaporated as I returned to the peace of Image Lake. The meadow was alive with marmots, fat, furry sentries whistling at my approach. Only two other people were camping by the outlet streams, a miracle in peak season. The low sun lit Glacier's western flanks, bathing the snow and ice with pale pink tints while the faintest of breezes rippled the surface of the lake, shivering the reflection. Tranquility poured into me, and the words clamoring in my brain fell silent. I heard only heart and breath.

This is the end of the grand crest. From here it rolls south, punctuated now and then by volcanoes or a brief flourish of rock and ice. After photographing the lake, I climbed back to the ridge top to gaze north once more to watch the dark peaks disappear into the night.

Right: *Heather finds some protection from the elements in a rocky crevice.*

Following page: *Looking toward the peaks of the Canadian border as the valleys fill with cloud.*

Photography Notes

I began fumbling with mountain photography in the late 1960s. After waiting days for my processed slides to arrive in the mail, I always felt a sting of disappointment as the carousel clicked around. My attempt to capture dazzling moments in the mountains had fallen short again. The 8-by-10 Cibachrome prints I made only highlighted my failings. Compared with the image I saw through my viewfinder, details smeared, colors dulled, and depth compressed. I aspired to achieve the grainless purity of an Ansel Adams print and the ravishing palette of Eliot Porter, but achieved little more than snapshots. What did the master photographers know that I didn't?

A lot, as it turns out. But their use of large-format cameras gave them an insuperable advantage. No amount of talent, skill, and care could compensate for the limitation of the tiny scrap of film in my 35 mm camera. Their 4-by-5-inch negatives and transparencies dwarfed my slides, which barely exceeded one square inch. To blow up the image on a 4-by-5 sheet of film to 8-by-10 increases the area by a factor of four. But the image on a 35 mm slide must grow eighty times larger to make the same-size print.

I considered moving to large format, but the prospect of lugging a 4-by-5 kit around the mountains didn't appeal. Ansel Adams often enlisted burros to haul his gear around the Sierras. Few trails snake through the high country of the North Cascades, and the jungles, chasms, and glaciers of the Lower 48's most rugged range are unsuited for pack animals. Large format was too cumbersome and 35 mm too limiting. I needed a happy medium.

Car enthusiasts used to say there's no substitute for cubic inches. Today, turbos and superchargers allow smaller engines to compete with the big boys. In photography, medium-format cameras coupled with the

Left: *This small tarn evaporates a few weeks after melting out.*

latest fine-grain emulsions rival 4-by-5 quality while retaining most of the convenience of 35 mm. I elected to try a Pentax 6-by-7 (6 by 7 centimeters), essentially a Schwarzeneggerian 35 mm that uses both 120 and 220 film to produce a 2-1/4 by 2-3/4-inch image. The Pentax, a hefty tripod, three lenses, and film weighed about twenty-five pounds. I would pack this weight, along with enough gear and food to stay out for a week at a time, and return with five hundred images. Many of the photos in this book come from those heavily laden trips.

Vibration is the enemy of clarity in any format, and I learned that the slow lenses, massive shutters, and extra weight of medium-format cameras magnifed the issue. I tried lightweight "backpacking" tripods. I used a shutter-release cable for long exposures. Locking up the viewfinder mirror before tripping the shutter sharpened the image, especially when using a telephoto lens, which multiplies the effects of vibration. Still, fuzzy images resulted with frustrating frequency. I reluctantly concluded only a heavy tripod and a sturdy ball head could dampen a shutter that opens with the impact of a guillotine. I found I could get away with lighter systems if I didn't extend the legs and if I draped weighted packs around the head, but the low placement limited my compositions. I resigned myself to one more burden, a heavy tripod. Adding ten or twelve pounds to an already heavy pack hurts, but losing your best shots to technical imperfections feels worse.

Unfortunately, groaning under such a burden drew the joy out of hiking. I tried the Pentax 645 for a while, but I saved little in weight and the smaller image didn't satisfy me. On my trip with Jim Nelson to Mount Challenger, Jim was using a Mamiya 645 (6 by 4.5 centimeters) rangefinder camera. He let me run a roll through it on the climb. I was hooked.

First, rangefinder cameras are light. Instead of viewing through the lens, a viewfinder has a separate viewer. The focus adjustment moves the lenses of both the viewfinder and the lens in tandem. Viewfinders save a few ounces by dispensing with the mirror and the machinery needed to swing it out of the way, which are found in most cameras. Viewfinder lenses of equivalent speed and focal length weigh less. And leaf shutters in the lenses themselves are tiny and cause almost no vibration, so skimpy tripods work fine. When Mamiya came out with the model 7 with the same 6-by-7 image size as my original Pentax, I had found my ideal camera.

Shortly after I began work on the North Cascades crest, Fuji introduced Velvia transparency film. Its fine grain rivaled Kodachrome, and its rendition of color, especially greens, appealed to me more than the old standard. As an E6 (Ektachrome) film, I could drop it at a local lab and pick it up in a few hours instead of shipping the rolls to out-of-state Kodak-approved facilities and waiting a week or more. Velvia has some competitors now, but almost every photograph in this book was shot on Velvia.

I carry only two or three filters. A graduated-split neutral-density filter is essential for limiting contrast at sunrise and sunset. As a wash of color brightens the twilight sky, the foreground will shift to black. Aligning the horizon with a split neutral-density filter that darkens the sky by two stops is enough to allow the film to register foreground details. I usually don't bother with a filter holder, preferring to hold the filter in one hand while triggering the shutter with the other.

I avoid circular split filters. They place the split in the middle of the scene thus dictating the composition.

Polarizing filters not only darken skies and cut through haze but also enhance color saturation. However, the latest emulsions already furnish ample saturation much of the time. Lately I've used polarizers to saturate the greens of wet leaves that would otherwise glare silver.

An 81A or 81B warming filter gets rid of blue shadows on clear days. I use them only for pale subjects that would otherwise pick up the cool blue.

A supersaturated film like Velvia demands truly neutral filters to deliver believable colors. Both my plastic Cokin split neutral-density filter and polarizer shift colors perceptibly toward magenta, where an equivalent Tiffen, B&W, or other glass filter seems more neutral. Given Velvia's sensitivity to nominally neutral filters, it can yield positively lurid results with colored filters, although warming filters judiciously employed can leach the blue out of shadows.

I had the good fortune to travel with Art Wolfe, by acclamation the world's most accomplished outdoor photographer. He selflessly taught me how he approaches photography. When, on our first trip together to Africa, I excitedly prepared to take a shot—of a sleeping lion, for example—I would check with Art, who usually shook his head, knowing my photograph was destined for the round file because of harsh light, a distracting background, or unbalanced composition. Most importantly, he taught me how film sees.

SUGGESTED READING

Alt, David D., and Donald W. Hyndman. *Northwest Exposures:
A Geologic Story of the Northwest*. Missoula: Mountain Press, 1995.

Beckey, Fred. *Cascade Alpine Guide: Climbing and High Routes,
Vol. 2: Stevens Pass to Rainy Pass*, 2nd ed. Seattle: The Mountaineers, 1989.

Beckey, Fred. *Cascade Alpine Guide: Climbing and High Routes,
Vol. 3: Rainy Pass to Fraser River*. 2nd ed. Seattle: The Mountaineers, 1995.

Beckey, Fred. *Challenge of the North Cascades*,
2nd ed. Seattle: The Mountaineers, 1996.

Crowder, D.F., and R. W. Tabor. *Routes and Rocks*. Seattle:
The Mountaineers, 1965.

Kerouac, Jack. *Desolation Angels*. Reissue ed. New York:
Riverhead Books, 1995.

Kerouac, Jack. *The Dharma Bums*. Reissue ed. New York: Penguin, 1991.

Mathews, Daniel. *Cascade-Olympic Natural History: A Trailside Reference*.
Portland: Raven Editions, with Portland Audubon Society, 1988.

Miles, John, ed. *Impressions of the North Cascades: Essays about a Northwest
Landscape*. Seattle: The Mountaineers, 1996.

Miller, Tom, and Harvey Manning. *The North Cascades*.
Seattle: The Mountaineers, 1964. O.P.

Nelson, Jim, and Peter Potterfield. *Selected Climbs in the Cascades*.
Seattle: The Mountaineers, 1993.

Snyder, Gary. *Earth House Hold: Technical Notes and Queries to Fellow Dharma
Revolutionaries*. New York: New Directions, 1969.

Snyder, Gary. *Riprap & Cold Mountain Poems*.
Reissue ed. New York: North Point Press, 1990.

Whalen, Philip. *Canoeing Up Cabarga Creek: Buddhist Poems 1955–1986*. Berkeley:
Parallax Press, 1996.